DEPARTMENT OF THE NAVY
HEADQUARTERS UNITED STATES MARINE CORPS
3000 MARINE CORPS PENTAGON
WASHINGTON, DC 20350-3000

I0426150

GROUND SAFETY SPECIALIST TRAINING AND READINESS MANUAL

DEPARTMENT OF THE NAVY
HEADQUARTERS UNITED STATES MARINE CORPS
3000 MARINE CORPS PENTAGON
WASHINGTON, DC 20350-3000

NAVMC DIR 3500.102
C 469
18 Jul 06

NAVMC DIRECTIVE 3500.102

From: Commandant of the Marine Corps
To: Distribution List

Subj: GROUND SAFETY SPECIALIST TRAINING AND READINESS MANUAL, (SHORT TITLE: GROUND SAFETY T&R MANUAL)

Ref: (a) MCO P3500.72A
      (b) MCO 1553.3A
      (c) MCRP 3-0A
      (d) MCO 1553.2A
      (e) MCRP 3-0B
      (f) MCO 3400.3F
      (g) MCO 1553.1B
      (h) MCO P1553.4A

1. Purpose. Per reference (a), this T&R Manual establishes training standards, regulations, and practices regarding the training of Marines and assigned Navy personnel who performing ground safety functions.

2. Information

   a. The training events in this Directive will be used to standardize unit training throughout the community, focus on Mission Essential Tasks (METs) for the community, and establish a framework for assessment of unit and individual training readiness. It includes individual training standards to be used by unit commanders and formal schools for the development of training plans, curricula, and records of training accomplished in order to establish a framework for identifying training achievements, training gaps, and objective assessments of readiness associated with the training of Marines.

   b. CG TECOM will update this T&R Manual as necessary to provide current and relevant training standards to commanders. Commanders will incorporate these training events into their training plans to the extent that the events support their unit's METs and time and other resources are available.

   c. All questions pertaining to the Marine Corps Ground T&R Program and Unit Training Management should be directed to: CG, TECOM (C 469), 1019 Elliot Road, Quantico, VA 22134.

3. Scope.

   a. Commanders will review, update, and submit unit Mission Essential Task Lists (METL) per references (b) and (c).

DISTRIBUTION STATEMENT A: Approved for public release; distribution is unlimited

b. Per reference (b), commanders shall conduct an internal assessment of the unit's ability to execute each MET and prepare a definitive plan of attack to achieve MET proficiency by developing long-, mid-, and short-range training plans to achieve proficiency in each MET.

c. Using this T&R Manual and other pertinent references, commanders will conduct evaluations (informal and formal) of their unit's ability to accomplish their METs. These training evaluations will be conducted at appropriate points in the unit's training cycle to determine MET proficiency and adjust training priorities.

d. Formal school directors and commanders will establish or review programs of instruction per reference (d) to ensure compliance with core individual training requirements as set forth in this Directive.

4. <u>Command</u>. This Directive is applicable to the Marine Corps Total Force.

5. <u>Certification</u>. Reviewed and approved this date.

K. J. STALDER
By direction

DISTRIBUTION: PCN 10303372300

Copy to: 7000260 (2)
         8145001 (1)

LOCATOR SHEET

Subj: GROUND SAFETY SPECIALIST TRAINING AND READINESS MANUAL, (SHORT TITLE:
        GROUND SAFETY T&R MANUAL)

Location: _____
                (Indicate location(s) of copy(ies) of this Directive.)

RECORD OF CHANGES

Log completed change action as indicated.

Change Number	Date of Change	Date Entered	Signature of Person Incorporated Change

GROUND SAFETY T&R MANUAL

TABLE OF CONTENTS

GROUND SAFETY T&R MANUAL

CHAPTER 1

OVERVIEW

GROUND SAFETY T&R MANUAL

CHAPTER 1

OVERVIEW

1000. INTRODUCTION

1. The Training and Readiness (T&R) Program is intended to become the Corps' primary tool for planning, conducting, evaluating training, and for assessing training readiness. The operating forces and supporting establishments have developed Mission Essential Task Lists (METLs) for ground communities using Marine Corps doctrine, Table of Organization (T/O) missions, Operational Plans, Contingency Plans, and Tactics, Techniques, and Procedures (TTP). T&R Manuals are built around these service-level METLs; all events contained in T&R Manuals relate directly back to this METL. The comprehensive T&R Program ensures the Marine Corps continue to improve its combat readiness by training more efficiently and effectively. Ultimately, this will enhance the Marine Corps' ability to accomplish all assigned missions.

2. The T&R Manual is a single document that seeks to capture the collective and individual training requirements to prepare units to accomplish their combat mission. The T&R Manual is not intended to be an encyclopedia that contains every minute detail of how to conduct training. Instead, it seeks to provide a framework, linked to a myriad of references, in order to provide a baseline to design, conduct, and assess training that prepares Marines to perform the mission. This manual is a fundamental tool for supervisors and commanders to build and maintain unit combat readiness. Using this tool, commanders can construct and execute an effective training plan that supports the unit's METL. More detailed information on the Marine Corps Ground T&R Program may be found in reference (a).

3. The T&R Manual is designed for use by curriculum developers to create courses of instruction and unit commanders to determine predeployment training requirements in preparation for training. This directive focuses on individual and collective tasks performed by opfor units and supervised by personnel in the performance of unit Mission Essential Tasks (METs).

1001. CORNERSTONE ORDERS

1. Guidance for training and evaluation in the Marine Corps, from entry-level training at the formal schools to advanced PME for senior enlisted and officers, is found in the cornerstone orders. All training and evaluation programs throughout the Marine Corps were designed using the guidance provided in these orders. The cornerstone orders are references (b), (d), (g), and (h).

1002. ORGANIZATION

1. This directive is written to support the Ground Safety training for operating force units. This directive is not intended to be a stand-alone

document. The Ground Safety Specialist staff will use this directive in conjunction with the references for each individual and collective event to train units to accomplish unit METs in these unique environments.

2. This directive is comprised of four chapters and two appendices. Chapter 2 contains the METs and the E-Coded events associated with those METs. Chapter 3 contains individual events. Appendix A is the terms and definitions commonly used in the Training and Readiness Program.

3. Individual training standards (Chapters 3) in this T&R Manual will contain at a minimum, the following elements:

    a. Event Code and Title

    b. Evaluation Code

    c. Sustainment Interval

    d. Event Description

    e. Event Condition

    f. Event Standard

    g. References

    h. Rank

As this directive evolves over time, additional event components may be added. Further discussion of event components is found in paragraph 1006 of this chapter.

1003. T&R EVENT CODING. T&R events are coded for ease of reference. Each event consists of a three-field designator; each field has up to 4 characters. The first field represents the MOS (8151) or Community (MCWO for Detachment). The second field represents the functional area of the event (e.g., WPNS for weapons; AT for Antiterrorism; etc.). The last field designates the level and sequence of the event. Figure (1) shows MCWO T&R levels and a sample MCWO T&R event. Event levels are categorized as 1000-level, 2000-level, and 3000-level. 1000-level events are individual core skills taught at the formal school. 2000-level events are core-plus skills taught at the formal school or managed on the job training (MOJT). An exception is the 8151-CMDC-2XXX events that are taught to detachment commanders only at the entry-level formal school. 3000-6000 level events are collective skills that are taught at MCMWTC and reinforced at the unit level when possible. Figure 1-1 provides a detail of MCWO T&R events and coding.

Individual Events Formal School 1000	Individual Events MOJT/Career Level School 2000	Collective Events Fire Team/Crew /Section 3000

Figure 1. T&R Event Levels

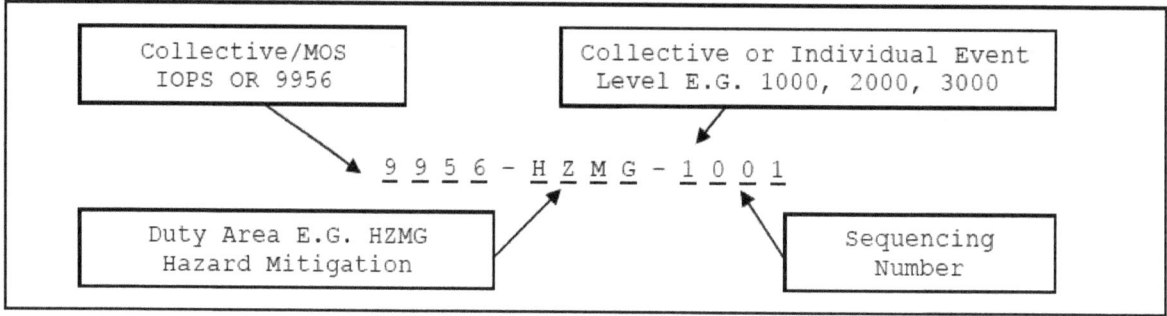

Figure 2. T&R Event Coding.

1004. EVALUATION-CODED (E-Coded) EVENTS

1. With limited time and material resources, it is imperative that commanders prioritize training to ensure their units are trained in those skills essential to accomplishing their mission. To assist with prioritization, certain events in the T&R Manual are Evaluation-Coded (E-Coded). Only significant events that are critical components of a MET or are key indicators of a unit's readiness are E-Coded. Only E-Coded events are used to calculate Combat Readiness Percentage (CRP) for each MET.

2. Per reference (d), all commanders in the operating forces are required to develop a unit METL based on the Universal Joint Task List (UJTL), Universal Navy Task List (UNTL), Marine Corps Task List (MCTL), doctrine, T/O mission statement, higher headquarters' METLs, contingency plans, and the assigned mission. The use of a METL-based training program allows the commander discretion in training and makes the T&R Manual a training tool rather than a prescriptive checklist.

3. This T&R Manual contains ITSs and CTSs that are unique to Ground Safety Specialist operations. Conduct of these operations will require individual skills from other functional areas (infantry, logistics, NBCD, first aid, communications, etc...). Only those skills deemed critical to Ground Safety training and readiness have been included in the T&R Manual. In order to eliminate redundancy in the T&R Ground Program, other non-critical common functional areas skills will not be included. Commanders and staff will refer to supporting T&R Manuals when developing training plans.

1005. COMBAT READINESS PERCENTAGE (CRP) CALCULATION

1. Ground Safety training shall be designed to accomplish the events that support the unit's ability to accomplish its METL, while simultaneously sustaining proficiency in individual core skills. The T&R Manual has events that directly support a MET. These events are E-Coded and are the only events that contribute toward unit CRP. This is done to assist commanders in prioritizing the training toward their unit's METL, taking into account resource, time, and personnel constraints.

2. Unit CRP increases after the completion of E-Coded events. The number of E-Coded events for the MET determines the value of each E-Coded event for that particular MET. All E-Coded events have equal value for CRP calculation. For example, if there are 4 E-Coded events for a MET, each is worth 25% of MET CRP. MET CRP is calculated by adding the percentage of each completed training event. The percentage for each MET is calculated the same way and all are added together and divided by the number of METS to determine CRP. For ease of calculation, we will say that each MET has 4 E-Coded events; each contributes 25% towards the completion of the MET. If the unit has completed and is current on three of the four E-Coded events for a given MET, then 75% of the MET is complete. The CRP for each MET is added together and divided by the number of METS to get the overall CRP. As an example using the MCWO T&R:

       MET 1: 75% complete (3 of 4 E-Coded events trained)
       MET 2: 71.43% complete (5 of 7 E-Coded events trained)
       MET 3: 100% complete (1 of 1 E-Coded event trained)
       MET 4: 75% complete (3 of 4 E-Coded events trained)

To derive CRP, simply add the CRP for each MET and divide by the number of METS:

MET CRP: 75 + 71.43 + 100 + 75 = 321.43

Ground Safety CRP: 321.43 (total MET CRP)/4 (total number of METS) = 80.36%

1006. T&R EVENT DETAIL

1. This section explains each of the elements of a T&R event. These are all the possible items that comprise an event. If a component is not applicable to a particular event, it is omitted.

    a. Event-Code. The event-code is a three-field character set. Each field will have up to 4 characters.

        (1) The first field indicates MOS off community (e.g., 9956).

        (2) The second field indicates functional or duty area (e.g., HZMG, ISPN, PLAN, etc...).

        (3) The third field indicates the level (1000 through 3000) and sequence (e.g., 001-999).

    b. Title. The name of the event.

c. <u>Evaluation-Coded</u>. This is a "yes/no" category indicating whether or not the event is E-Coded. If yes, the event contributes toward CRP of the associated MET. The value of each E-Coded event is based on number of E-Coded events for that MET. Refer to Section 1004 for a more detailed explanation of E-Coded events.

d. <u>Supported MET(s)</u>. List all METs that are supported by the training event.

e. <u>Sustainment Interval</u>. This is the period, expressed in number of months, between evaluation and retraining requirements. Skills and capabilities acquired through the accomplishment of training events are to be refreshed at pre-determined intervals. It is essential that these intervals be adhered to in order to ensure the unit and Marines of the unit maintain proficiency.

f. <u>Billet</u>. Each individual training event will contain a billet code that designates who (by billet) is responsible for performing that event and any corresponding formal course required for that billet. Each commander has the flexibility to shift responsibilities based on the organization of his command. These codes are based on recommendations from the collective subject matter expertise that developed the manual and are listed for each event.

g. <u>Grade</u>. The rank at which Ground Safety Specialists are required to complete the event.

h. <u>Description</u>. Description of event purpose, goals, objectives, and requirements. It is a general description of an action requiring learned skills and knowledge, e.g., perform guard mount post and relief.

i. <u>Condition</u>. The conditions set for real world or combat situation in which the task is to be performed. They indicate what is provided (equipment, tools, materials, manuals, aids, etc...), environmental constraints or conditions under which the task is performed, and any specific cues or indicators to which the performer must respond. When resources or safety requirements limit the conditions, this should be stated.

j. <u>Standard</u>. The performance standard indicates the basis for judging the effectiveness of the performance. It consists of a carefully worded statement that identifies the proficiency level expected when the task is performed. The standard provides the minimum acceptable performance parameters and must be strictly adhered to. The standard for collective events will likely be general, describing the desired end-state or purpose of the event. The standard for individual events will more specifically describe to what proficiency level, specified in terms of accuracy, speed, sequencing, quality of performance, adherence to procedural guidelines, etc..., the event is to be accomplished.

k. <u>Event Components</u>. Description of the actions that the event is composed of, or a list of subordinate, included T&R event codes, and event descriptions. The event components help the user determine what must be accomplished and to properly plan for the event.

l. Prerequisite Events. Prerequisites are academic training or other T&R events that must be completed prior to attempting the task. They are lower-level events or tasks that give the individual/unit the skills required to accomplish the event. They can also be planning steps, administrative requirements, or specific parameters that build toward mission accomplishment.

m. Chained Events. Collective T&R events are supported by lower-level collective and individual T&R events. This enables unit leaders to identify subordinate T&R events that ultimately support specific mission essential tasks. When the accomplishment of any upper-level events, by their nature, result in the performance of certain subordinate and related events, the events are "chained." The completion of chained events will update sustainment interval credit (and CRP for E-Coded events) for the related subordinate level events.

n. Related ITSs. A list of all the Individual Training Standards that support the event.

o. References. The training references shall be used to determine task performance steps, grading criteria, and ensure standardization of training procedures. They assist the trainee in satisfying the performance standards, or the trainer in evaluating the effectiveness of task completion. Since T&R Manuals provide only a training outline, references are key to developing lesson plans and adding specificity, such as performance steps, related doctrine, or other detailed information.

p. Distance Learning Products. Individual Multimedia Instruction (IMI), Computer-Based Training (CBT), Marine Corps Institute (MCI), etc. Included when the event can be taught via one of these media methods vice attending a formal course of instruction or receiving MOJT.

q. Support Requirements. This is a list of the external and internal support the unit and Marines will need to complete the event. This is a key section in the overall T&R effort, as resources will eventually be tied directly to the training towards METS. Future efforts to attain and allocate resources will be based on the requirements outlined in the T&R Manual. The list includes, but is not limited to:

    (1) Range(s)/Training Area

    (2) Equipment

    (3) Materials

    (4) Other Units/Personnel

r. Miscellaneous. Any additional information that will assist in the planning and execution of the event. The list may include, but is not limited to:

    (1) Admin Instructions

    (2) Special Personnel Certifications

      (3) Equipment Operating Hours

2. Future revisions of this directive may incorporate additional event components as applicable.

1007. UNIT TRAINING

1. The unit's training program emphasizes qualifications and the overall combat readiness of the unit. Individual T&R events are the building blocks for overall unit readiness, however, unit training should take priority over training of a select, few individuals. Integration of individual and collective training events into the unit-training plan is essential. Commanding Officers will ensure that this training philosophy is implemented. Unit training must predominate, and units must tailor their training plans to ensure combat readiness. Commanders should rely upon the expertise of Ground Safety personnel when conducting Ground Safety training. Reliance upon Ground Safety personnel, adherence to the policies contained in the references, and use of this directive constitutes a solid foundation for unit training.

2. The training of Marines to perform as an integrated unit in combat lies at the heart of the T&R program. Unit readiness and individual readiness are directly related. Individual training and the mastery of individual core skills serve as the building blocks for unit combat readiness. A Marine's ability to perform critical skills required in combat is essential, however, it is not necessary to have all individuals within an organization fully trained in order for that organization to accomplish its assigned tasks. Manpower shortfalls, temporary assignments, leave, or other factors outside the commander's control, often affect the ability to conduct individual training. Regardless of current manning, the unit must maintain the ability to accomplish its assigned mission.

3. Commanders shall ensure that all tactical training is conducted to a T&R collective standard. The T&R manual is the unit training standard, and all training events shall support the unit METL and be tailored to meet T&R standards.

4. Commanders shall provide personnel the opportunities to attend formal and operational level courses of instruction as required by reference (e). Attendance at all formal courses must enhance the warfighting capabilities of the unit.

1008. REQUIREMENTS FOR COLLECTIVE TRAINING. Collective training shall serve to achieve standards of unit proficiency required to accomplish wartime missions. Subject to such constraints as safety requirements and limits on space for training, all collective training shall be conducted under conditions and rates of activity closely approximating those that the units being trained may encounter in combat. When constraints limit the use of realistic training conditions, then simulation and other products of training technology shall be used as applicable to enhance realism. Collective training, to the degree feasible, shall include electronic warfare activity; nuclear, biological, and chemical defense activity; and the periodic use of opposing forces trained in the tactics of potential adversaries. All

collective training exercises shall emphasize realistic performance of the functions of individual personnel in the exercising units. Support units shall be integrated into exercises for realistic training in their wartime supporting roles.

1009. NUCLEAR, BIOLOGICAL, CHEMICAL (NBC) TRAINING

1. All personnel assigned to the operating force must be trained in NBCD in order to survive and continue their mission in an NBC environment. Individual proficiency standards are defined as survival and basic operating standards. Survival standards are those that the individual must master in order to survive NBC attacks. Basic operating standards are those that the individual, and collectively the unit, must be capable of performing to continue operations in an NBC environment. In order to develop and maintain the ability to operate in an NBC environment, NBC training should be an integral part of the training plan and events in this directive should be trained under NBC conditions whenever possible.

2. NBCD officers and specialists are instrumental in integrating realistic scenarios/situations that challenge units' ability to operate in an NBC environment.

3. Further guidance on NBCD training is found in reference (f).

1010. NIGHT TRAINING. While it is understood that all personnel and units of the operating force must be capable of performing their assigned mission in "every clime and place," current doctrine emphasizes the requirement to perform assigned missions at night and during periods of limited visibility. Basic skills are significantly more difficult when visibility is limited. To ensure units are capable of accomplishing their mission at night as well as during the day, they must train under the more difficult limited visibility conditions. As such, all events in this directive should be conducted during the day and at night or under conditions of limited visibility. When there is limited training time available, night training should be conducted in lieu of day training.

1011. APPLICATION OF SIMULATION. Simulators and other training devices for weapon systems and equipment shall be used when they are capable of effectively and economically supplementing training on the actual equipment. Particular emphasis shall be placed on simulators that provide training that might be limited by safety considerations or constraints on training space, time, or other resources. When deciding on simulation issues, the primary consideration shall be improving the quality of training and consequently the state of readiness. Potential savings in operating and support costs normally shall be an important secondary consideration.

1012. UNIT TRAINING MANAGEMENT

1. Unit training management (UTM) is the application of the Marine Corps Training Principles and the Systems Approach to Training to satisfy the training requirements of commanders at all levels in order to accomplish

their wartime mission. Guidance for UTM and the process for establishing effective UTM programs are contained in references (c), (d), and (e). These references are the basis for the development of this directive. Familiarity with (c) will enhance understanding of the Systems Approach to Training (SAT) process used in METL development and Marine Corps UTM principles.

2. UTM focuses training on the tasks that are essential to a unit's wartime capabilities. The SAT process provides commanders with the requisite tools and techniques to analyze, design, develop, implement, and evaluate the training of their unit. The Marine Corps training principles provide sound and proven direction and are flexible enough to accommodate the demands of local conditions. These principles are not inclusive, nor do they guarantee success. They are guides that commanders can use to manage unit-training programs. The Marine Corps training principles are:

    a. Train as you fight,

    b. Make commanders responsible for training,

    c. Use standards-based training,

    d. Use performance-oriented training,

    e. Use mission-oriented training,

    f. Train the MAGTF to fight as a combined arms team,

    g. Train to sustain proficiency, and

    h. Train to challenge.

3. To maintain an efficient, effective training program, it is imperative that commanders at every level fully understand and implement UTM. Further guidance and other training resources can be found on the UTM website at http://www.tecom.usmc.mil/utm/.

1013. TRAINING EVALUATION

1. The purpose of formal and informal evaluation is to provide commanders with a process to determine a unit's proficiency in the tasks it must successfully perform in combat. Informal evaluations should be conducted during every training evaluation. Formal evaluations are often scenario-based, focused on the unit's METs, based on collective training standards, and usually conducted during higher-level collective events.

2. Evaluation is a continuous process. Evaluation is integral to training management and is conducted by leaders at every level and during all phases of the planning and conduct of training. Training evaluations measure individual and collective ability to perform events specified in this directive. To ensure Ground Safety training is efficient and effective, it is imperative that evaluation be an integral part of the training plan. References (a), (c), and (e) provide further guidance on the conduct of informal and formal evaluations.

1014. OPERATIONAL RISK MANAGEMENT (ORM). ORM is a process that enables commanders to plan for and minimize risk while still accomplishing the mission. It is a decision making tool used by Marines at all levels to increase operational effectiveness by anticipating hazards and reducing the potential for loss, thereby increasing the probability of a successful mission. ORM minimizes risks to acceptable levels, commensurate with mission accomplishment. Commanders, leaders, maintainers, planners, and schedulers shall integrate risk assessment in the decision-making process and implement hazard controls to reduce risk to acceptable levels. Applying the ORM process will reduce mishaps, lower costs, and provide for more efficient use of resources. ORM assists the commander in conserving lives and resources and avoiding unnecessary risk, making an informed decision to implement a course of action (COA), identifying feasible and effective control measures where specific measures do not exist, and providing reasonable alternatives for mission accomplishment. Most importantly, ORM assists the commander in determining the balance between training realism and unnecessary risks in training, the impact of training operations on the environment, and the adjustment of training plans to fit the level of proficiency and experience of Marines and leaders. Further guidance for ORM can be found in reference (a).

1015. CAREER PROFESSIONAL READING. Marines must continue to strive for excellence in all they do. The career professional reading lists contained in each chapter are finite examples developed by the SMEs who developed this manual of the vast array of materials available for professional and career development. These voluntary reading materials are included to augment core training and help to improve the proficiency of formal school and detachment staff.

1016. CONCLUSION. The Marine Corps Ground T&R Program continues to evolve. The vision for this program is that it will link the Uniform Joint Task List (UJTL), the Uniform Navy Task List (UNTL), and the Marine Corps Task List (MCTL) to METLs and unit training. In doing so, it will tie all training and training resources directly to unit missions. The Defense Readiness Reporting System (DRRS) is currently being developed and encompasses Enhanced Status of Resources and Training System (ESORTS). The purpose of this system is to measure and report on the readiness of military forces and the supporting infrastructure to meet missions and goals assigned by the Secretary of Defense. Training readiness in DRRS will be based primarily on METs. Because unit CRP is based on the unit's training towards its METs, it will provide a more accurate picture of a unit's ability to accomplish its mission. This will give fidelity to future funding requests and factor into the allocation of resources. Additionally, the Ground T&R Program will help to ensure training remains focused on mission accomplishment and that training readiness reporting is tied to commanders' METLs.

GROUND SAFETY T&R MANUAL

CHAPTER 2

MISSION ESSENTIAL TASKS

2000. MISSION ESSENTIAL TASK LIST. The list below includes Mission Essential Task List that support each MET.

MET 1. Mitigate hazards	
9956-HZMG-1001	Conduct unit range operations
9956-HZMG-1002	Establish a Lockout/Tagout (LOTO) Program
9956-HZMG-1003	Establish a program to prevent or minimize off-duty and recreation mishaps
9956-HZMG-1004	Execute radiofrequency radiation hazards program (non-ionizing)
9956-HZMG-1005	Execute USMC hearing conservation program
9956-HZMG-1006	Execute unit material handling equipment (MHE) safety program
9956-HZMG-1007	Execute a HAZCOM program
9956-HZMG-1008	Execute a laser safety control program
9956-HZMG-1009	Execute a command/unit asbestos and lead program
9956-HZMG-1010	Execute a confined space entry program
9956-HZMG-1011	Execute a fall protection program
9956-HZMG-1012	Execute a fire safety program
9956-HZMG-1013	Execute an office safety program
9956-HZMG-1014	Execute bloodborne pathogen program
9956-HZMG-1015	Execute ergonomic program
9956-HZMG-1016	Execute the Marine Corps explosive safety program
9956-HZMG-1017	Facilitate an industrial hygiene program
9956-HZMG-1018	Execute the Marine Corps traffic safety program
9956-HZMG-1019	Execute the Marine Corps' respiratory protection program
9956-HZMG-1020	Execute the sight conservation program (SCP)
9956-HZMG-1021	Maintain personal protective equipment
9956-HZMG-1022	Execute electrical safety program
9956-HZMG-1023	Execute ionizing radiation control program
MET 2. Plan unit response	
9956-PLAN-1041	Develop disaster plans
9956-PLAN-1042	Develop emergency action plans
9956-PLAN-1043	Develop pre-mishap plans
MET 3. Report mishaps	
9956-RPRT-1051	Execute the USMC Mishap Investigation and Reporting Program
9956-RPRT-1052	Use the web enabled safety system (WESS)
MET 4. Implement commands safety program	
9956-TRNG-1061	Implement a unit safety program
MET 5. Inspect units	
9956-INSP-1031	Manage unit safety inspection program
9956-INSP-1032	Perform Operational Risk Management (ORM)

GROUND SAFETY T&R MANUAL

CHAPTER 3

GROUND SAFETY INDIVIDUAL EVENTS

GROUND SAFETY T&R MANUAL

CHAPTER 3

GROUND SAFETY INDIVIDUAL EVENTS

3000. PURPOSE. This chapter includes all individual training events for the Ground Safety Specialist. An individual training standard is an event that a Ground Safety Specialist would perform at a unit or installation. These events are linked to a service-level Mission Essential Tasks (METs). This linkage tailor individual training for the selected MET. Each individual training standard provides an event title, along with the conditions events will be performed under, and the standard to which the event must be performed to be successful.

3001. ADMINISTRATIVE NOTES

1. T&R events are coded for ease of reference. Each event has a 4-4-4 character identifier. The first four characters are "9956" for Ground Safety Specialist. The second four characters represent the functional area of ground safety. The last four characters are the level of training and sequential numbering. Functional area descriptions are as follows:

   A. HZMG – Hazard Mitigation. These behaviors relate to the Ground Safety Specialist responsibilities to execute the various unit safety programs required by Marine Corps orders, Navy directives, and OSHA regulations. The Ground Safety Specialist does not draft these programs, but advises the commander regarding the necessary programs, and takes certain actions relating to these necessary programs.

   B. INSP – Inspection. Marine Corps orders, Navy directives, and OSHA regulations require that organizations periodically inspect their workplaces for safety related concerns.

   C. PLAN – Planning. Marine Corps operation orders contain safety plans which the Ground Safety Specialist must draft.

   D. RPRT – Reporting. All serious mishaps must be reported up the chain of command in a specific format using a specific reporting system.

   E. TRNG – Training. The Ground Safety Specialist has the responsibility to inculcate his entire unit with a holistic approach to safety which encompasses advising the commander, executing the various programs, training the unit, and various administrative functions.

2. All events in this manual can be accomplished with or without the aid of references.

3002. INDEX OF INDIVIDUAL TRAINING EVENTS

1. **1000 - Level Individual Events.** Basic Ground Training Safety Specialist individual events taught during initial MOS formal school training.

EVENT	DESCRIPTION	PAGE
MET 1	**Mitigate hazards**	
9956-HZMG-1001	Conduct unit range operations	3-5
9956-HZMG-1002	Establish a Lockout/Tagout (LOTO) Program	3-5
9956-HZMG-1003	Establish a program to prevent or minimize off-duty and recreation mishaps	3-6
9956-HZMG-1004	Execute radiofrequency radiation hazards program (non-ionizing)	3-7
9956-HZMG-1005	Execute USMC hearing conservation program	3-7
9956-HZMG-1006	Execute unit material handling equipment (MHE) safety program	3-8
9956-HZMG-1007	Execute a HAZCOM program	3-9
9956-HZMG-1008	Execute a laser safety control program	3-9
9956-HZMG-1009	Execute a command/unit asbestos and lead program	3-10
9956-HZMG-1010	Execute a confined space entry program	3-11
9956-HZMG-1011	Execute a fall protection program	3-11
9956-HZMG-1012	Execute a fire safety program	3-12
9956-HZMG-1013	Execute an office safety program	3-13
9956-HZMG-1014	Execute bloodborne pathogen program	3-13
9956-HZMG-1015	Execute ergonomic program	3-14
9956-HZMG-1016	Execute the Marine Corps explosive safety program	3-15
9956-HZMG-1017	Facilitate an industrial hygiene program	3-15
9956-HZMG-1018	Execute the Marine Corps traffic safety program	3-16
9956-HZMG-1019	Execute the Marine Corps' respiratory protection program	3-16
9956-HZMG-1020	Execute the sight conservation program (SCP)	3-17
9956-HZMG-1021	Maintain personal protective equipment	3-18
9956-HZMG-1022	Execute electrical safety program	3-18
9956-HZMG-1023	Execute ionizing radiation control program	3-19
MET 2	**Plan unit response**	
9956-PLAN-1041	Develop disaster plans	3-21
9956-PLAN-1042	Develop emergency action plans	3-21
9956-PLAN-1043	Develop pre-mishap plans	3-22
MET 3	**Report mishaps**	
9956-RPRT-1051	Execute the USMC Mishap Investigation and Reporting Program	3-23
9956-RPRT-1052	Use the web enabled safety system (WESS)	3-24

MET 4	Implement commands safety program	
9956-TRNG-1061	Implement a unit safety program	3-24
MET 5	Inspect units	
9956-INSP-1031	Manage unit safety inspection program	3-20
9956-INSP-1032	Perform Operational Risk Management (ORM)	3-20

3003. INDIVIDUAL EVENTS

9956-HZMG-1001: Conduct unit range safety operations

EVALUATION-CODED: NO   **SUSTAINMENT INTERVAL:** 24 months

DESCRIPTION: Safe range operations are dependent on the following factors: facilities that permit complete control and security of the range, operating procedures founded on safe practices, personnel fully qualified and trained in all facets of range safety, and the knowledgeable cooperation of the personnel on the range.

GRADES: CPL, SSGT, GYSGT, 1STSGT, MSGT, 2NDLT, 1STLT, CAPT, MAJ

INITIAL TRAINING SETTING: FORMAL

CONDITION: Given a range, and a mission to train personnel in marksmanship related activities

STANDARD: So that there are no negligent discharges and no personnel are injured or killed.

PERFORMANCE STEPS:
1. Identify who has authority to waive safety criteria.
2. Ensure OIC and the RSO on a live fire range know their responsibilities.
3. Ensure that ammunition is stored as required on a firing range.
4. Identify the personnel authorized to lead munitions range clearance operations.
5. Ensure proper ammunition issuing procedures are enforced on a firing range.
6. Ensure proper disposal of materials involved in malfunctions.
7. Review a range safety plan.

REFERENCES:
1. MCO 3570.1B Policies and Procedures for Firing Ammunition for Training, Target Practice and Combat
2. MCO 3571.2F Explosive Ordnance Disposal (EOD) Procedures

9956-HZMG-1002: Establish a Lockout/Tagout (LOTO) Program

EVALUATION-CODED: NO   **SUSTAINMENT INTERVAL:** 24 months

DESCRIPTION: "Lockout/Tagout (LOTO)" refers to specific practices and procedures to safeguard employees from the unexpected energization or startup of machinery and equipment, or the release of hazardous energy during service or maintenance activities. This requires that a designated individual turn off and disconnect the machinery or equipment from its energy source(s) before performing service or maintenance, and that the authorized employee(s) either lock or tag the energy-isolating device(s) to prevent the release of hazardous energy and take steps to verify that the energy has been isolated effectively.

GRADES: CPL, SGT, SSGT, GYSGT, MSGT, 1STSGT, 2NDLT, 1STLT, CAPT, MAJ

INITIAL TRAINING SETTING: FORMAL

CONDITION: Given powered machinery or equipment.

STANDARD: So that no machinery or equipment ever starts or releases energy unexpectedly.

PERFORMANCE STEPS:
1. Execute an energy control program.
2. Draft a written Lockout/Tagout Plan.
3. Identify when machinery/equipment needs to be LOTO.
4. Identify the equipment not covered in the LOTO Program.

REFERENCES:
1. 29 CFR 1910.133 Occupational Safety and Health Standards - Eye and face protection
2. 29 CFR 1910.147 Occupational Safety and Health Standards - The control of hazardous energy (lockout/tagout)
3. NAVMC Dir 5100.1 Marine Corps Ground Occupational Safety and Health Program

---

9956-HZMG-1003: Establish a program to prevent or minimize off-duty and recreation mishaps

EVALUATION-CODED: NO   **SUSTAINMENT INTERVAL**: 24 months

DESCRIPTION: Marine Corps units establish procedures to eliminate or minimize the probability of mishaps occurring during off-duty and/or activities. Commanders at all levels are responsible for the planning and execution of command sponsored and Marine Corps Community Services (MCCS) sponsored off-duty and recreational programs and activities that incorporate risk management to lower the risk presented by off-duty and recreational opportunities.

GRADES: CPL, SGT, SSGT, GYSGT, MSGT, 1STSGT, 2NDLT, 1STLT, CAPT, MAJ

INITIAL TRAINING SETTING: FORMAL

CONDITION: Given personnel who participate in off duty activities and recreation.

STANDARD: So that no personnel are injured or killed.

PERFORMANCE STEPS:
1. Brief the commander on his responsibilities for implementing and maintaining an effective program.
2. Access resources.

REFERENCE:
1. MCO 5100.30A Marine Corps Off-Duty and Recreation Safety Program

---

9956-HZMG-1004: Execute radiofrequency radiation hazards program (non-ionizing)

EVALUATION-CODED: NO   **SUSTAINMENT INTERVAL:** 12 months

DESCRIPTION: Radiation from radio-frequency (RF) transmitters has the potential to directly injure the soft tissue of personnel who are near the radiating antennas. These injuries result from the tissue being cooked in a manner similar to the way food is cooked in a microwave oven. Transmitters aboard ships, on aircraft, and at shore stations are potential sources of harmful radiation. This task mitigates the danger from these radiation sources.

GRADES: CPL, SGT, SSGT, GYSGT, MSGT, 1STSGT, 2NDLT, 1STLT, CAPT, MAJ

INITIAL TRAINING SETTING: FORMAL

CONDITION: Given a unit with potential exposure to harmful RF transmissions.

STANDARD: To prevent all injuries from radiation exposure.

PERFORMANCE STEPS:
1. Post Radio Frequency Radiation warning signs.
2. Identify the hazards associated with Radio Frequency Radiation.
3. Brief the command on the elements that make up the RFR Program.
4. Identify who must receive Radio Frequency Radiation training.
5. Identify a unit Radiation Safety Officer.

REFERENCES:
1. DoDI 6055.11A Protection of DoD Personnel from Exposure to Radiofrequency Radiation and Military Exempt Lasers
2. MCO 5104.2 Marine Corps Radiofrequency Electromagnetic Field Personnel Protection Program
3. Mil-STD 882B System Safety Program Requirements

9956-HZMG-1005: Execute USMC hearing conservation program

EVALUATION-CODED: NO   **SUSTAINMENT INTERVAL:** 24 months

DESCRIPTION: Although noise-induced hearing loss is one of the most common occupational illnesses, it is often ignored because there are no visible effects, it usually develops over a long period of time, and, except in very rare cases, there is no pain. What does occur is a progressive loss of communication, socialization, and responsiveness to the environment. This task mitigates the effect of loud workplace noises on the hearing of a unit's personnel.

GRADES: CPL, SGT, SSGT, GYSGT, 1STSGT, 2NDLT, 1STLT, CAPT, MAJ

INITIAL TRAINING SETTING: FORMAL

CONDITION: Given a unit with exposure to loud noises, in a garrison or field environment.

STANDARD: To prevent all personnel from suffering hearing loss.

PERFORMANCE STEPS:
1. Identify noise hazards.
2. Ensure personnel have appropriate hearing protection.
3. Execute recommended risk mitigation factors.
4. Identify supporting Industrial Hygienist.

REFERENCES:
1. 29 CFR 1910.95 Occupational Safety and Health Standards - Occupational noise exposure
2. MCO 6260.1E Marine Corps Hearing Conservation Program

9956-HZMG-1006: Execute unit material handling equipment (MHE) safety program

EVALUATION-CODED: NO   **SUSTAINMENT INTERVAL**: 12 months

DESCRIPTION: Material handling equipment (MHE), are mechanical devices for handling of supplies with greater ease and economy. MHE refers to various materials handling equipment, to include but not limited to forklifts, shelf pickers, motorized pallet jacks (hand trucks), tractors, and other specialized industrial trucks powered by electric motors or internal combustion engines. Safety practices for Powered Material-Handling Equipment (MHE) will be followed and the operators will be trained in the use of equipment. Operators will be trained on the safe and efficient operation of the equipment and will pass all physical, aptitude, and licensing examinations required.

GRADES: CPL, SGT, SSGT, GYSGT, MSGT, 1STSGT, 2NDLT, 1STLT, CAPT, MAJ

INITIAL TRAINING SETTING: FORMAL

CONDITION: Given a unit with MHE, in a garrison or field environment.

STANDARD: To prevent injury or death to personnel based on MHE mishap.

PERFORMANCE STEPS:
1. Ensure operators are trained to MHE standards.
2. Establish a timetable for operator refresher training.
3. Recognize the safe parameters for operating MHE.
4. Conduct MHE pre-use inspection.
5. Determine the maximum lifting capacity of MHE.

REFERENCES:
1. 29 CFR 1910 Occupational Safety and Health Standards.
2. 29 CFR 1915 Occupational Safety and Health Standards for Shipyard Employment
3. 29 CFR 1917 Marine Terminals
4. 29 CFR 1918 Safety and Health Regulations for Longshoring
5. 29 CFR 1926 Safety and Health Regulations for Construction
6. NAVSEA SW023-AH-WHM-010 Handling Ammunition and Explosives with Industrial Material Handling Equipment (MHE)

9956-HZMG-1007: Execute a HAZCOM program

EVALUATION-CODED: NO   **SUSTAINMENT INTERVAL:** 12 months

DESCRIPTION: A HAZCOM plan must be prepared for all persons who handle, store, use, process, dispose of or might possibly be exposed to hazardous materials, or may be exposed to hazardous materials in the conduct of their job.

GRADES: CPL, SGT, SSGT, GYSGT, MSGT, 1STSGT, 2NDLT, 1STLT, CAPT, MAJ

INITIAL TRAINING SETTING: FORMAL

CONDITION: Given a unit with the possibility of exposure to hazardous wastes.

STANDARD: To minimize all exposures to hazardous material and to protect employees from the health risks associated with hazardous materials.

PERFORMANCE STEPS:
1. Brief the command on the program responsibilities.
2. Ensure HAZCOM containers are labeled.
3. Ensure Material Safety Data Sheets (MSDS) are readily available.
4. Ensure the unit is trained in HAZCOM.
5. Provide for proper storage.
6. Ensure hazardous materials are disposed of properly.
7. Ensure spills are cleaned up.
8. Develop emergency response procedures.
9. Ensure work practice controls and PPE requirements are developed and implemented by supervisors.
10. Communicate applicable information to affected unit personnel.

REFERENCES:
1. 29 CFR 1910.1030 Occupational Safety and Health Standards - Bloodborne pathogens
2. 29 CFR 1910.120 Occupational Safety and Health Standards - Hazardous waste operations and emergency response
3. 29 CFR 1910.1200 Occupational Safety and Health Standards - Hazard communication
4. NAVMC Dir 5100.1 Marine Corps Ground Occupational Safety and Health Program
5. Local Base Order

9956-HZMG-1008: Execute a laser safety control program

EVALUATION-CODED: YES   **SUSTAINMENT INTERVAL:** 24 months

DESCRIPTION: Lasers can cause damage to the eye in a very short period of time. It is critical that all those who work with or around Lasers utilize protective eyewear and follow established safety guidelines. If improperly used or controlled, lasers can produce injuries (including burns, blindness, or electrocution) to operators and other personnel, including uninitiated visitors to laboratories, and cause significant damage to property. Individual users of all lasers must be adequately trained to ensure full understanding of the safety practices. This behavior relies on general familiarity with laser safety but does not qualify the Marine as a Laser Safety Officer.

GRADES: CPL, SGT, SSGT, GYSGT, MSGT, 1STSGT, 2NDLT, 1STLT, CAPT, MAJ

INITIAL TRAINING SETTING: FORMAL

CONDITION: Given a unit with equipment utilizing lasers, in a garrison or field environment.

STANDARD: To prevent injuries, blindness, and death resulting from improper use of laser equipment.

PERFORMANCE STEPS:
1. Ensure personnel working with lasers have appropriate PPE.
2. Identify personnel who are required to be enrolled in a medical surveillance program.
3. Post warning signs associated with lasers.
4. Identify Laser Safety Officer as a POC.

REFERENCES:
1. ANSI Z136.1-2000 American National Standard for the Safe Use of Lasers
2. EO410-BA-GYD-010 Technical Manual, Laser Safety
3. MCO 5104.1B Marine Corps Laser Hazard Control Program
4. MIL-HDBK 828A Laser Range Safety

9956-HZMG-1009: Execute a command/unit asbestos and lead program.

EVALUATION-CODED: NO   **SUSTAINMENT INTERVAL:** 24 months

DESCRIPTION: Construction materials containing asbestos and lead-based paint were commonly used in older buildings. The prevalence and adverse health affects associated with exposure to these materials has prompted the enactment of numerous public safety regulations. Asbestos and lead exposure have numerous, detrimental health effects for the respiratory and pulmonary systems which can result in death.

GRADES: CPL, SGT, SSGT, GYSGT, MSGT, 1STSGT, 2NDLT, 1STLT, CAPT, MAJ

INITIAL TRAINING SETTING: FORMAL

CONDITION: Given a unit with possible exposure to asbestos or lead, in a garrison or field environment.

STANDARD: To prevent any exposure or infestation of lead or asbestos.

PERFORMANCE STEPS:
1. Recognize possible sources of lead and asbestos.
2. Ensure workers have appropriate PPE for working with lead and asbestos.
3. Post warning signage used for lead and asbestos work areas.
4. Brief command on the potential hazards associated with working with asbestos and lead.
5. Ensure proper housekeeping for working with lead and asbestos.
6. Execute recommended mitigation measures.

REFERENCES:
1. 29 CFR 1910.1001 Occupational Safety and Health Standards - Asbestos
2. 29 CFR 1910.1025 Occupational Safety and Health Standard - Lead
3. 29 CFR 1926.1101 Safety and Health Regulations for Construction - Asbestos
4. 29 CFR 1926.62 Safety and Health Regulations for Construction - Lead
5. NAVMC Dir 5100.1 Marine Corps Ground Occupational Safety and Health Program

---

9956-HZMG-1010: Execute a confined space entry program.

EVALUATION-CODED: NO   **SUSTAINMENT INTERVAL:** 24 months

DESCRIPTION: A confined space is defined as any location that has limited openings for entry and egress, is not intended for continuous employee occupancy, and is so enclosed that natural ventilation may not reduce air contaminants to levels below the Threshold Limit Value (TLV). Examples of confined spaces include: manholes, stacks, pipes, storage tanks, trailers, tank cars, pits, sumps, hoppers, refuelers, aircraft, and bins. Entry into confined spaces without the proper precautions could result in injury and/or impairment or death.

GRADES: CPL, SGT, SSGT, GYSGT, MSGT, 1STSGT, 2NDLT, 1STLT, CAPT, MAJ

INITIAL TRAINING SETTING: FORMAL

CONDITION: Given a unit with exposure to confined spaces.

STANDARD: To prevent injury or death in confined spaces.

PERFORMANCE STEPS:
1. Maintain a list of organizational confined spaces.
2. Recognize confined spaces.
3. Identify Confined Spaces Program Manager.

REFERENCES:
1. 29 CFR 1910.146 Occupational Safety and Health Standards - Confined Spaces
2. NAVAIR 01-1A-35 Maintenance Instructions for Organizational, Intermediate and Depot Level Aviation Fuel Cells and Tanks
3. NAVMC Dir 5100.1 Marine Corps Ground Occupational Safety and Health Program
4. NAVSEA S6470-AA-SAF-010 Gas Free Engineering Manual

9956-HZMG-1011: Execute a fall protection program.

EVALUATION-CODED: NO   **SUSTAINMENT INTERVAL:** 12 months

DESCRIPTION: The purpose of this fall protection program is to establish guidelines to protect all personnel engaged in outdoor or indoor work activities that expose them to potential falls from elevations. This fall protection program includes all buildings and personnel. In particular those personnel engaged in work activities which expose them to falls from heights of 6 feet or more.

GRADES: CPL, SGT, SSGT, GYSGT, MSGT, 1STSGT, 2NDLT, 1STLT, CAPT, MAJ

INITIAL TRAINING SETTING: FORMAL

CONDITION: Given a unit with exposure to the potential for falls from six feet or higher, in a garrison or field environment.

STANDARD: To prevent injury or death resulting from a fall.

PERFORMANCE STEPS:
1. Recognize hazardous areas as they relate to fall protection.
2. Advise the commander on potential fall hazards.
3. Ensure appropriate portable and extension ladders are used.

REFERENCES:
1. 29 CFR 1910 Subpart D Walking-Working Surfaces
2. 29 CFR 1926 Safety and Health Regulations for Construction
3. NAVMC Dir 5100.1 Marine Corps Ground Occupational Safety and Health Program

---

9956-HZMG-1012: Execute a fire safety program.

EVALUATION-CODED: NO   SUSTAINMENT INTERVAL: 24 months

DESCRIPTION: The unit should ensure personnel are trained in regards to fire hazards in the workplace and what to do in a fire emergency. If the unit prefers personnel to evacuate, they must be trained on how to escape. If personnel will use firefighting equipment, there must be appropriate equipment and training to use the equipment safely.

GRADES: CPL, SGT, SSGT, GYSGT, MSGT, 1STSGT, 2NDLT, 1STLT, CAPT, MAJ

INITIAL TRAINING SETTING: FORMAL

CONDITION: Given a unit, in garrison or field environment.

STANDARD: So that no injuries or death result from a fire.

PERFORMANCE STEPS:
1. Brief the unit on the requirements of the fire safety program.
2. Ensure the unit is trained regarding general fire safety.
3. Ensure extinguishers are inspected as required.
4. Identify emergency response personnel.
5. Post appropriate fire signage.

REFERENCES:
1. 29 CFR 1910.156 Fire brigades
2. 29 CFR 1910.157 Portable fire extinguishers
3. 29 CFR 1910.37 Maintenance, safeguards, and operational features for exit routes
4. 29 CFR 1910.39 Fire prevention plans
5. MCO 11320.1J Fire Regulations
6. NFPA 101 Life Safety Code

9956-HZMG-1013: Execute an office safety program

EVALUATION-CODED: NO   **SUSTAINMENT INTERVAL:** 24 months

DESCRIPTION: Despite common beliefs that the office provides a safe environment in which to work, many hazards exist which can cause injury and health problems each year among personnel in office spaces. Since a substantial number of Marine Corps personnel works in offices, even low rates of work-related injuries and illnesses can have an immense impact on personnel safety and health.

GRADES: CPL, SGT, SSGT, GYSGT, MSGT, 1STSGT, 2NDLT, 1STLT, CAPT, MAJ

INITIAL TRAINING SETTING: FORMAL

CONDITION: In a unit with personnel performing work in offices.

STANDARD: To prevent all hazardous conditions.

PERFORMANCE STEPS:
1. Survey office spaces for safety concerns.
2. Evaluate office spaces for safety concerns.
3. Recommend mitigation for safety concerns.

REFERENCE:
1. NAVMC Dir 5100.1 Marine Corps Ground Occupational Safety and Health Program

---

9956-HZMG-1014: Execute a bloodborne pathogen program

EVALUATION-CODED: NO   **SUSTAINMENT INTERVAL:** 24 months

DESCRIPTION: An infection control plan must be prepared for all persons who handle, store, use, process, and disposes of or might possibly be exposed to infectious medical wastes, or may foreseeably be exposed to blood, body fluids in the conduct of their job.

GRADES: CPL, SGT, SSGT, GYSGT, MSGT, 1STSGT, 2NDLT, 1STLT, CAPT, MAJ

INITIAL TRAINING SETTING: FORMAL

CONDITION: Given a unit with the possibility of exposure to bloodborne pathogens.

STANDARD: To minimize all exposure to bloodborne pathogens and to protect employees from the health risks associated with bloodborne pathogens.

PERFORMANCE STEPS:
1. Brief the command on program responsibilities.
2. Ensure bloodborne pathogen containers are labeled.
3. Ensure the command is trained to handle bloodborne pathogens.
4. Ensure bloodborne pathogens are disposed of properly.
5. Ensure spills are cleaned up.
6. Develop emergency response procedures.

7. Develop work practice controls and PPE requirements.
8. Execute work practice controls and PPE requirements.
9. Communicate applicable information to effected unit personnel.

REFERENCES:
1. 29 CFR 1910.1030 Occupational Safety and Health Standards - Bloodborne pathogens
2. NAVMC Dir 5100.1 Marine Corps Ground Occupational Safety and Health Program

---

9956-HZMG-1015: Execute ergonomic program

EVALUATION-CODED: NO   **SUSTAINMENT INTERVAL:** 24 months

DESCRIPTION: Musculoskeletal and nervous disorders are a family of muscular conditions that result from repeated motions performed in the course of normal work or daily activities. Musculoskeletal and nervous disorders include carpal tunnel syndrome, bursitis, tendonitis, epicondylitis, ganglion cyst, tenosynovitis, and trigger finger. Musculoskeletal and nervous disorders are caused by too many uninterrupted repetitions of an activity or motion, unnatural or awkward motions such as twisting the arm or wrist, overexertion, incorrect posture, or muscle fatigue. This behavior requires the application of standard ergonomic principles. Ergonomic injuries are often described by the term "musculoskeletal disorders" or "MSDs." This is the term of art in scientific literature that refers collectively to a group of injuries and illnesses that affect the musculoskeletal system.

GRADES: CPL, SGT, SSGT, GYSGT, MSGT, 1STSGT, 2NDLT, 1STLT, CAPT, MAJ

INITIAL TRAINING SETTING: FORMAL

CONDITION: In a unit with personnel performing repeated motions in the course of normal work activities, in a garrison or field environment.

STANDARD: To prevent the loss of any work time.

PERFORMANCE STEPS:
1. Recognize musculoskeletal and nervous disorders.
2. Apply administrative controls to reduce musculoskeletal and nervous disorders.
3. Apply engineering controls to reduce musculoskeletal and nervous disorders.
4. Ensure command personnel are trained to reduce musculoskeletal and nervous disorders.
5. Ensure proper ergonomic maintenance of facility, equipment and tools.

REFERENCES:
1. NAVMC Dir 5100.1 Marine Corps Ground Occupational Safety and Health Program
2. OPNAVINST 5100.23G Navy Occupational Safety and Health (SOH) Program Manual

---

9956-HZMG-1016: Execute the Marine Corps explosive safety program.

EVALUATION-CODED: NO   **SUSTAINMENT INTERVAL:** 12 months

DESCRIPTION: Explosive handlers and maintainers often become complacent in dealing with explosives and related systems. There is an absolute need to constantly re-emphasize the inherent dangers and procedures in dealing with explosives. Explosive handlers need 100% inventory accuracy, security, and reporting. An aggressive explosives safety and accident prevention program will essentially help to prevent injuries and damage to equipment and potentially save lives.

GRADES: CPL, SGT, SSGT, GYSGT, MSGT, 1STSGT, 2NDLT, 1STLT, CAPT, MAJ

INITIAL TRAINING SETTING: FORMAL

CONDITION: Given a unit which uses, stores, transports or otherwise has exposure to explosives, in a garrison or field environment.

STANDARD: To prevent injury or death as a result of an explosives mishap.

PERFORMANCE STEPS:
1. Brief the command on policies for Marine Corps ammunition management and explosive safety.
2. Ensure that net explosive weight limits of ammunition storage on a firing range are not exceeded.
3. Monitor the Explosive Driver Program.

REFERENCES:
1. MCO 3570.1B Policies and Procedures for Firing Ammunition for Training, Target Practice and Combat
2. MCO 3571.2F Explosive Ordnance Disposal (EOD) Procedures
3. MCO 8020.10 USMC Ammo & Explosives Safety Policy
4. MCO 8023.3A Personnel Qualification and Certification Program for Class V Ammunition and Explosives
5. NAVSEA OP 5, VOL 1 Ammunition and Explosives Ashore Safety Regulations for Handling, Storing, Production, Renovation and Shipping
6. NAVSEA OP 5, VOL 3 Ammunition and Explosives Ashore; Advanced Bases
7. OPNAVINST 5530.13 DON Physical Security Instruction for Conventional Arms, Ammunition, and Explosives

---

9956-HZMG-1017: Facilitate an industrial hygiene program

EVALUATION-CODED: NO   **SUSTAINMENT INTERVAL:** 24 months

DESCRIPTION: Industrial hygiene is the anticipation, recognition, evaluation, and control of job-site hazards and exposures that may result in injury or illness to personnel.

GRADES: CPL, SGT, SSGT, GYSGT, MSGT, 1STSGT, 2NDLT, 1STLT, CAPT, MAJ

INITIAL TRAINING SETTING: FORMAL

CONDITION: Given a unit, in a garrison or field environment.

STANDARD: To identify all hazards and exposures at all times.

PERFORMANCE STEPS:
1. Evaluate the unit for industrial hygiene concerns.
2. Monitor the unit for factors of industrial hygiene in the workplace.
3. Facilitate an exposure survey.
4. Ensure affected personnel are added to the Medical Surveillance Program.
5. Implement recommendations.

REFERENCES:
1. NAVMC Dir 5100.1 Marine Corps Ground Occupational Safety and Health Program
2. OPNAVINST 5100.23G Navy Occupational Safety and Health Program Manual

9956-HZMG-1018: Execute the Marine Corps traffic safety program

EVALUATION-CODED: NO   SUSTAINMENT INTERVAL: 12 months

DESCRIPTION: The purpose of the program is to identify traffic safety problem areas and implement programs to reduce the number and severity of vehicular crashes through the Marine Corps wide traffic safety program. The program also encourages all safe use of the roadways by vehicular or pedestrian traffic.

GRADES: CPL, SGT, SSGT, GYSGT, MSGT, 1STSGT, 2NDLT, 1STLT, CAPT, MAJ

INITIAL TRAINING SETTING: FORMAL

CONDITION: Given a unit which uses government vehicles or has personnel with privately owned vehicles, in a garrison or field environment.

STANDARD: To prevent injury or death due to a traffic mishap.

PERFORMANCE STEPS:
1. Brief the Marine Corps Traffic Safety Policy.
2. Brief the requirements of the Drive Safe Program.
3. Facilitate the Safe Driving Council.
4. Execute the Drive Safe Program.
5. Execute the Driver Education Program.
6. Train personnel on the PPE requirements for motorcycles.
7. Execute the Motor Vehicle Inspection Program.

REFERENCES:
1. DoDI 6055.1 DoD Safety and Occupational Health (SCH) Program
2. MCO 5100.19E Marine Corps Traffic Safety Program (Drive safe)

9956-HZMG-1019: Execute the Marine Corps's respiratory protection program

EVALUATION-CODED: NO   SUSTAINMENT INTERVAL: 24 months

DESCRIPTION: It is the policy of the Marine Corps to provide personnel with a safe respiratory working environment. This is accomplished by utilizing facilities and equipment that have all feasible respiratory safeguards incorporated into their design. When effective engineering controls are not feasible, or when they are being initiated, respiratory protection shall be used to ensure personnel protection.

GRADES: CPL, SGT, SSGT, GYSGT, MSGT, 1STSGT, 2NDLT, 1STLT, CAPT, MAJ

INITIAL TRAINING SETTING: FORMAL

CONDITION: Given a unit with exposure to potential respiratory hazards, in a garrison or field environment.

STANDARD: To prevent injury or death due to inhalation of a toxic substance.

PERFORMANCE STEPS:
1. Draft the Commander's written respiratory Protection Program.
2. Determine if medical surveillance is required.
3. Execute recommended mitigation measures.
4. Arrange fit test.
5. Ensure proper storage and maintenance of respiratory equipment.
6. Coordinate training for respiratory users.
7. Ensure shops procure correct respiratory equipment.

REFERENCES:
1. ANSI Z88.2 Practices for Respiratory Protection
2. NAVMC Dir 5100.1 Marine Corps Ground Occupational Safety and Health Program

---

9956-HZMG-1020: Execute the sight conservation program (SCP)

EVALUATION-CODED: NO   **SUSTAINMENT INTERVAL:** 24 months

DESCRIPTION: The Marine Corps Sight Conservation Program identifies eye hazard situations, posts those hazards, and provides personal eye protection.

GRADES: CPL, SGT, SSGT, GYSGT, MSGT, 1STSGT, 2NDLT, 1STLT, CAPT, MAJ

INITIAL TRAINING SETTING: FORMAL

CONDITION: Given a unit with exposure to potential eye injuries, in a garrison or field environment.

STANDARD: To prevent eye injury or blindness.

PERFORMANCE STEPS:
1. Brief the command on the Marine Corps's policy on sight conservation.
2. Identify eye hazard operation area using industrial hygiene evaluation.
3. Post signs in eye hazard area.
4. Ensure unit has appropriate eye protection.
5. Ensure medical surveillance for personnel that work in an eye hazard area.
6. Recognize causal factors for the most common types of eye injuries.
7. Maintain plumbed and portable eye wash stations.
8. Draft PPE requirements for a visitor entering an eye hazard area.
9. Train personnel working in an eye hazard area.
10. Execute recommended mitigation measures.
11. Ensure appropriate maintenance and storage of eye PPE.

REFERENCES:
1. 29 CFR 1910.132 Occupational Safety and Health Standards - Personal Protective Equipment General Requirements
2. 29 CFR 1910.133 Occupational Safety and Health Standards - Eye and face protection
3. ANSI Z358.1-1990 Emergency Eye Wash and Shower Equipment
4. ANSI Z87.1-1989 Practice for Occupational/Educational Eye and Face Protection
5. NAVMC Dir 5100.1 Marine Corps Ground Occupational Safety and Health Program

---

9956-HZMG-1021: Maintain personal protective equipment

EVALUATION-CODED: NO   **SUSTAINMENT INTERVAL:** 24 months

DESCRIPTION: The importance of PPE involves the selection, maintenance, and use of PPE; the training of employees; and monitoring the equipment to ensure its ongoing effectiveness.

GRADES: CPL, SGT, SSGT, GYSGT, MSGT, 1STSGT, 2NDLT, 1STLT, CAPT, MAJ

INITIAL TRAINING SETTING: FORMAL

CONDITION: In a unit that employs PPE, in a garrison or field environment, in sanitary conditions.

STANDARD: To prevent loss or compromise of PPE.

PERFORMANCE STEPS:
1. Inspect PPE.
2. Maintain PPE.
3. Brief the command on its responsibilities as they relate to PPE.
4. Inventory PPE.
5. Communicate basic program requirements to employees.
6. Facilitate certification of PPE, as appropriate.

REFERENCES:
1. 29 CFR 1910.132 Occupational Safety and Health Standards - Personal Protective Equipment General Requirements
2. NAVMC Dir 5100.1 Marine Corps Ground Occupational Safety and Health Program

---

9956-HZMG-1022: Execute the electrical safety program

EVALUATION-CODED: NO   **SUSTAINMENT INTERVAL:** 12 months

DESCRIPTION: Electricity has long been recognized as a serious workplace hazard, exposing employees to electric shock, electrocution, burns, fires, and explosions. Hazards exist in the exposed or operating elements of an electrical installation such as lighting, equipment, motors, machines, appliances, switches, controls, and enclosures, so these items must be constructed and installed to minimize workplace electrical dangers. Certain approved testing organizations test and certify electrical equipment before use in the workplace to ensure they are safe.

GRADES: CPL, SGT, SSGT, GYSGT, MSGT, 1STSGT, 2NDLT, 1STLT, CAPT, MAJ

INITIAL TRAINING SETTING: FORMAL

CONDITION: In a unit with electrical equipment, in a garrison or field environment.

STANDARD: So that all electrical hazards are identified.

PERFORMANCE STEPS:
1. Brief command on identified hazards.
2. Ensure personnel working on energized equipment have required PPE.
3. Recognize common hazards associated with electrical equipment.
4. Submit appropriate work request to address hazardous conditions.
5. Document hazards.

REFERENCES:
1. 29 CFR 1910 Subpart S Electrical
2. 29 CFR 1926 Safety and Health Regulations for Construction
3. NAVMC Dir 5100.1 Marine Corps Ground Occupational Safety and Health Program
4. NFPA 70 National Electrical Code
5. SPAWARINST 5100.9D Navy Shore Electronics Safety Precautions

---

9956-HZMG-1023: Execute ionizing radiation control program

EVALUATION-CODED: NO   **SUSTAINMENT INTERVAL:** 24 months

DESCRIPTION: Ionizing radiation sources can be found in a wide range of occupational settings, including health care facilities, research institutions, nuclear reactors and their support facilities, nuclear weapon production facilities, and other various manufacturing settings, just to name a few. These radiation sources can pose a considerable health risk to affected workers if not properly controlled.

INITIAL TRAINING SETTING: FORMAL

CONDITION: Given a unit with exposure to sources of non-ionizing radiation, in a garrison or field environment.

STANDARD: To prevent all injuries, blindness and death to unit personnel.

PERFORMANCE STEPS:
1. Post warning signage at all non-ionizing radiation sites.
2. Ensure welding curtains are available.
3. Ensure face shields are available.

REFERENCES:
1. 29 CFR 1910.252 General requirements - Welding, Cutting, and Brazing
2. OPNAVINST 5100.23G Navy Occupational Safety and Health (SOH) Program Manual

---

9956-INSP-1031: Manage unit safety inspection program

EVALUATION-CODED: NO   **SUSTAINMENT INTERVAL**: 12 months

DESCRIPTION: Focused safety inspection is expected to include an assessment of physical hazards. Other potential serious hazards that come to the inspector's attention during the course of the inspection must also be addressed and documented. All workplaces must be inspected annually.

GRADES: CPL, SGT, SSGT, GYSGT, MSGT, 1STSGT, 2NDLT, 1STLT, CAPT, MAJ

INITIAL TRAINING SETTING: FORMAL

CONDITION: Given a unit, in a garrison or field environment.

STANDARD: To detect all unsafe conditions or situations.

PERFORMANCE STEPS:
1. Document discrepancies.
2. Recognize most frequently cited violations.
3. Observe hazards.
4. Respond to an Unsafe/Unhealthful Notice.
5. Provide recommendations for mitigation.
6. Evaluate hazards.
7. Conduct annual inspections.
8. Brief commander on inspection results.
9. Maintain inspection records.

REFERENCES:
1. 29 CFR 1910.1903 Abatement Verification
2. 29 CFR 1926.22 Safety and Health Regulations for Construction - Recording and reporting of injuries
3. MCO 5100.29A Marine Corps Safety Program
4. NAVMC 11400 OSH Deficiency Notice
5. NAVMC Dir 5100.1 Marine Corps Ground Occupational Safety and Health Program

---

9956-INSP-1032: Perform Operational Risk Management (ORM)

EVALUATION-CODED: NO   **SUSTAINMENT INTERVAL**: 12 months

DESCRIPTION: ORM is a decision-making tool to systematically help identify operational risks and benefits and determine the best courses of action for any given situation. ORM is performed during operational use. This risk management process, as well as other safety risk management processes, is designed to minimize risks in order to reduce mishaps, preserve assets, and safeguard the health and welfare of personnel.

GRADES: CPL, SGT, SSGT, GYSGT, MSGT, 1STSGT, 2NDLT, 1STLT, CAPT, MAJ

INITIAL TRAINING SETTING: FORMAL

CONDITION: In a garrison or field environment.

STANDARD: In every situation, at all times.

PERFORMANCE STEPS:
1. Brief the command on ORM.
2. Apply the Five Steps of Risk Management.
3. Utilize the Risk Assessment worksheet.
4. Utilize basic hazard identification tools.
5. Facilitate ORM assessment.
6. Train unit in ORM.
7. Ensure ORM is incorporated into all plans, orders and activities.

REFERENCES:
1. FM 100-14 Risk Management
2. MCO 3500.27B Operational Risk Management

9956-PLAN-1041: Develop disaster plans

EVALUATION-CODED: NO   **SUSTAINMENT INTERVAL:** 12 months

DESCRIPTION: Our personnel are the Marine Corps' most important and valuable asset. Put procedures in place before a disaster, and prepare for what personnel need to recover after a disaster. Ensure the well-being of personnel's family members, recognizing that getting back to work is important to the recovery of those who have experienced disasters. It is important to re-establish routines, when possible.

GRADES: CPL, SGT, SSGT, GYSGT, MSGT, 1STSGT, 2NDLT, 1STLT, CAPT, MAJ

INITIAL TRAINING SETTING: FORMAL

CONDITION: Given a mission.

STANDARD: During the planning process, in the time allotted by the commanding officer.

PERFORMANCE STEPS:
1. Incorporate safety concerns into planning process.
2. Identify hazards.
3. Assess possibility of mitigating hazards.
4. Identify necessary warning times.
5. Draft safety portion of operational order, as appropriate.
6. Brief recommended mitigations.

REFERENCES:
1. MCO 5100.1 Marine Corps OSH Program
2. NAVMC Dir 5100.1 Marine Corps Ground Occupational Safety and Health Program

---

9956-PLAN-1042: Develop emergency action plans

EVALUATION-CODED: NO   **SUSTAINMENT INTERVAL:** 12 months

DESCRIPTION: An emergency action plan describes the actions personnel should take to ensure their safety if a fire or other emergency situation occurs. Well developed emergency plans and proper employee training (such that personnel understand their roles and responsibilities within the plan) will result in fewer and less severe employee injuries and less structural damage to the facility during emergencies. A poorly prepared plan, likely will lead to a disorganized evacuation or emergency response, resulting in confusion, injury, and property damage.

GRADES: CPL, SGT, SSGT, GYSGT, MSGT, 1STSGT, 2NDLT, 1STLT, CAPT, MAJ

INITIAL TRAINING SETTING: FORMAL

CONDITION: Given a mission.

STANDARD: During the planning process, in the time allotted by the commanding officer.

PERFORMANCE STEPS:
1. Incorporate safety concerns into the planning process.
2. Identify hazards.
3. Assess likelihood of mitigating hazards.
4. Identify warning time necessary.
5. Draft safety portion of the operational order, as appropriate.
6. Include the locations/telephone numbers of emergency response teams.
7. Include identification and location of emergency devices.
8. Include notification lists of persons/offices to be contacted.
9. Include lists of persons/offices (with phone numbers) of chain of command.
10. Include provision for a means of secondary emergency communications.
11. Include procedures for emergency operation or shutdown of equipment.
12. Brief recommended mitigations.

REFERENCES:
1. MCO 5100.1 Marine Corps OSH Program
2. NAVMC Dir 5100.1 Marine Corps Ground Occupational Safety and Health Program

---

9956-PLAN-1043: Develop pre-mishap plan

EVALUATION-CODED: NO   **SUSTAINMENT INTERVAL:** 24 months

DESCRIPTION: A pre-mishap plan describes - in advance - the steps that must be taken when a mishap occurs. Anticipate all reasonable eventualities and devise measures to cope with them. Deficiencies may be identified through periodic drills designed to ensure the plan's smooth execution when a mishap occurs.

INITIAL TRAINING SETTING: FORMAL

CONDITION: Given a unit.

STANDARD: During the planning process, in the time allotted by the commanding officer.

PERFORMANCE STEPS:
1. Incorporate safety concerns into the planning process.
2. Identify hazards.
3. Assess the possibility to mitigate hazards.
4. Identify necessary warning times.
5. Draft safety portion of the operational order, as appropriate.
6. Brief recommended mitigations.

REFERENCES:
1. MCO 3500.27B Operational Risk Management
2. MCO 5102.1B Mishap Investigation, Reporting and Record-keeping

---

9956-RPRT-1051: Execute the USMC Mishap Investigation and Reporting Program

EVALUATION-CODED: NO   **SUSTAINMENT INTERVAL:** 24 months

DESCRIPTION: To establish and implement comprehensive programs to investigate, report, and keep related records on accidental death, injury, occupational illness, and property damage for accidents and prescribe and enforce regulations directly related to investigation, reporting, and keeping records on accidental death, injury, occupational illness, and property damage.

GRADES: CPL, SGT, SSGT, GYSGT, MSGT, 1STSGT, 2NDLT, 1STLT, CAPT, MAJ

INITIAL TRAINING SETTING: FORMAL

CONDITION: Given a unit or a Security Investigation Board.

STANDARD: To investigate every accident involving unit personnel or equipment.

PERFORMANCE STEPS:
1. Brief the command on the responsibilities of all persons involved with mishap reporting.
2. Recognize when a Safety Investigation Board SIB is required.
3. Report mishaps to appropriate authority.
4. Maintain mishap information at the unit level.
5. Conduct mishap investigation.
6. Conduct trend analysis.
7. Brief lessons learned.
8. Provide mishap data to commanding officer.
9. Endorse SIB reports, when required.
10. Maintain on and off duty mishap log.
11. Safeguard privileged information.
12. Dispose of privileged information, as appropriate.
13. Develop pre-mishap plan developed and implemented.

REFERENCES:
1. DoDI 6055.7 Accident Investigation, Reporting, and Record Keeping
2. MCO 5100.1 Marine Corps OSH Program
3. MCO 5100.29A Marine Corps Safety Program
4. MCO P5102.1B Navy and Marine Corps Mishap And Safety Investigation Reporting, And Record Keeping Manual

5. NAVMC Dir 5100.1 Marine Corps Ground Occupational Safety and Health Program
6. SECNAVINST 5100.10H Department Of The Navy Policy For Safety, Mishap Prevention, Occupational Health And Fire Protection Manual

---

9956-RPRT-1052: Use the web enabled safety system (WESS).

EVALUATION-CODED: NO   **SUSTAINMENT INTERVAL**: 12 months

DESCRIPTION: The Web-Enabled Safety System (WESS), with complete, on-line mishap reporting and data retrieval for non-aviation mishaps, went "live" July 12, 2004. It simplifies and brings the field and fleet mishap- and hazard-reporting procedures and safety data analysis into 21st century. It is a major improvement over its predecessor, WESS 1, and all previous PC-based and naval message-reporting methods.

GRADES: CPL, SGT, SSGT, GYSGT, MSGT, 1STSGT, 2NDLT, 1STLT, CAPT, MAJ

INITIAL TRAINING SETTING: FORMAL

CONDITION: Given a reportable mishap.

STANDARD: Within eight hours of receiving mishap data.

PERFORMANCE STEPS:
1. Gather data.
2. Input timely hazard data.
3. Extract reports.
4. Input accurate hazard data.

REFERENCE:
1. MCO 5102.1B Mishap Investigation, Reporting and Record-keeping

---

9956-TRNG-1061: Implement a unit safety program.

EVALUATION-CODED: NO   **SUSTAINMENT INTERVAL**: 12 months

DESCRIPTION: All the element of the Marine Safety Program must be imparted to all Marines so that all are aware of the hazards and their responsibilities.

GRADES: CPL, SGT, SSGT, GYSGT, MSGT, 1STSGT, 2NDLT, 1STLT, CAPT, MAJ

INITIAL TRAINING SETTING: FORMAL

CONDITION: Given a unit, in a garrison or field environment.

STANDARD: To train all personnel.

PERFORMANCE STEPS:
1. Advise commander regarding safety related matters.
2. Execute programs.
3. Inspect unit for safety.

4. Plan the units' response to incidents.
5. Brief unit on safety.

REFERENCES:
1. NAVMC Dir 5100.1 Marine Corps Ground Occupational Safety and Health Program

GROUND SAFETY T&R MANUAL

APPENDIX A

TERMS AND DEFINITIONS

Terms in this glossary are subject to change as applicable orders and directives are revised. Terms established by Marine Corps orders or directives take precedence after definitions found in Joint Pub 1-02, *DoD Dictionary of Military and Associated Terms.*

A

After Action Review. A professional discussion of training events conducted after all training to promote learning among training participants. The formality and scope increase with the command level and size of the training evolution. For longer exercises, they should be planned for at predetermined times during an exercise. The results of the AAR shall be recorded on an after action report and forwarded to higher headquarters. The commander and higher headquarters use the results of an AAR to reallocate resources, prioritize their training plan, and plan for future training.

Assessment. An informal judgment of the unit's proficiency and resources made by a commander or trainer to gain insight into the unit's overall condition. It serves as the basis for the midrange plan. Commanders make frequent use of these determinations during the course of the combat readiness cycle in order to adjust, prioritize or modify training events and plans.

C

Chaining. A process that enables unit leaders to effectively identify subordinate collective events and individual events that support a specific collective event. For example, collective training events at the 4000-level are directly supported by collective events at the 3000-level. Utilizing the building block approach to progressive training, these collective events are further supported by individual training events at the 1000 and 2000-levels. When a higher-level event by its nature requires the completion of lower level events, they are "chained"; Sustainment credit is given for all lower level events chained to a higher event.

Collective Event. A clearly defined, discrete, and measurable activity, action, or event (i.e., task) that requires organized team or unit performance and leads to accomplishment of a mission or function. A collective task is derived from unit missions or higher-level collective tasks. Task accomplishment requires performance of procedures composed of supporting collective or individual tasks. A collective task describes the exact performance a group must perform in the field under actual operational conditions. The term "collective" does not necessarily infer that a unit accomplishes the event. A unit, such as a squad or platoon conducting an attack; may accomplish a collective event or, it may be accomplished by an individual to accomplish a unit mission, such as a battalion supply officer completing a reconciliation of the battalion's CMR. Thus, many collective events will have titles that are the same as individual events; however, the standard and condition will be different because the scope of the collective event is broader.

Collective Training Standards (CTS). Criteria that specify mission and functional area unit proficiency standards for combat, combat support, and combat service support units. They include tasks, conditions, standards, evaluator instruction, and key indicators. CTS are found within collective training events in T&R Manuals.

Combat Readiness Cycle. The combat readiness cycle depicts the relationships within the building block approach to training. The combat readiness cycle progresses from T&R Manual individual core skills training, to the accomplishment of collective training events, and finally, to a unit's participation in a contingency or actual combat. The combat readiness cycle demonstrates the relationship of core capabilities to unit combat readiness. Individual core skills training and the training of collective events lead to it proficiency and the ability to accomplish the unit's stated mission.

Combat Readiness Percentage (CRP). The CRP is a quantitative numerical value used in calculating collective training readiness based on the E-coded events that support the unit METL. CRP is a concise measure of unit training accomplishments. This numerical value is only a snapshot of training readiness at a specific time. As training is conducted, unit CRP will continuously change.

Component Events. Component events are the major tasks involved in accomplishing a collective event. Listing these tasks guide Marines toward the accomplishment of the event and help evaluators determine if the task has been done to standard. These events may be lower-level collective or individual events that must be accomplished.

Condition. The condition describes the training situation or environment under which the training event or task will take place. Expands on the information in the title by identifying when, where, and why the event or task will occur and what materials, personnel, equipment, environmental provisions, and safety constraints must be present to perform the event or task in a real-world environment. Commanders can modify the conditions of the event to best prepare their Marines to accomplish the assigned mission (e.g. in a desert environment; in a mountain environment; etc.)

Core Competency. Core competency is the comprehensive measure of a unit's ability to accomplish its assigned MET. It serves as the foundation of the T&R Program. Core competencies are those unit core capabilities and individual core skills that support the commander's METL and T/O mission statement. Individual competency is exhibited through demonstration of proficiency in specified core tasks and core plus tasks. Unit proficiency is measured through collective tasks.

Core Capabilities. Core capabilities are the essential functions a unit must be capable of performing during extended contingency/combat operations. Core unit capabilities are based upon mission essential tasks derived from operational plans; doctrine and established tactics; techniques and procedures.

Core Plus Capabilities. Core plus capabilities are advanced capabilities that are environment, mission, or theater specific. Core plus capabilities may entail high-risk, high-cost training for missions that are less likely to be assigned in combat.

Core Plus Skills. Core plus skills are those advanced skills that are environment, mission, rank, or billet specific. 2000-level training is designed to make Marines proficient in core skills in a specific billet or at a specified rank at the Combat Ready level. 3000-8000-level training produces combat leaders and fully qualified section members at the Combat Qualified level. Marines trained at the Combat Qualified level are those the commanding officer feels are capable of accomplishing unit-level missions and of directing the actions of subordinates. Many core plus tasks are learned via MOJT, while others form the base for curriculum in career level MOS courses taught by the formal school.

Core Skills. Core skills are those essential basic skills that "make" a Marine and qualify that Marine for an MOS. They are the 1000-level skills introduced in entry-level training at formal schools and refined in operational units.

D

Defense Readiness Reporting System (DRRS). A comprehensive readiness reporting system that evaluates readiness on the basis of the actual missions and capabilities assigned to the forces. It is a capabilities-based, adaptive, near real-time reporting system for the entire Department of Defense.

Deferred Event. A T&R event that a commanding officer may postpone when in his or her judgment, a lack of logistic support, ammo, ranges, or other training assets requires a temporary exemption. CRP cannot be accrued for deferred "E-coded" events.

Delinquent Event. An event becomes delinquent when a Marine or unit exceeds the sustainment interval for that particular event. The individual or unit must update the delinquent event by first performing all prerequisite events. When the unit commander deems that performing all prerequisite is unattainable, then the delinquent event will be re-demonstrated under the supervision of the appropriate evaluation authority.

E

E-coded Event. An "E-coded" event is a collective T&R event that is a noted indicator of capability or, a noted Collective skill that contributes to the unit's ability to perform the supported MET. As such, only "E-coded" events are assigned a CRP value and used to calculate a unit's CRP.

Entry-level training. Pipeline training that equips students for service with the Marine Operating Forces.

Evaluation. Evaluation is a continuous process that occurs at all echelons, during every phase of training and can be both formal and informal. Evaluations ensure that Marines and units are capable of conducting their combat mission. Evaluation results are used to reallocate resources, reprioritize the training plan, and plan for future training.

Event (Training). (1) An event is a significant training occurrence that is identified, expanded and used as a building block and potential milestone for a unit's training. An event may include formal evaluations. (2) An event within the T&R Program can be an individual training evolution, a collective training evolution or both. Through T&R events, the unit commander ensures that individual Marines and the unit progress from a combat capable status to a Fully Combat Qualified (FCQ) status.

Event Component. The major procedures (i.e., actions) that must occur to perform a Collective Event to standard.

Exercise Commander (EC). The Commanding General, Marine Expeditionary Force or his appointee will fill this role, unless authority is delegated to the respective commander of the Division, Wing, or FSSG. Responsibilities and functions of the EC include:

(1) Designate unit(s) to be evaluated,
(2) May designate an exercise director,
(3) Prescribe exercise objectives and T&R events to be evaluated,
(4) Coordinate with commands or agencies external to the Marine Corps and adjacent Marine Corps commands, when required.

Exercise Director (ED). Designated by the EC to prepare, conduct, and report all evaluation results. Responsibilities and functions of the ED include:

(1) Publish a letter of instruction (LOI) that: delineates the T&R events to be evaluated, establishes timeframe of the exercise, lists responsibilities of various elements participating in the exercise, establishes safety requirements/guidelines, and lists coordinating instructions.
(2) Designate the TEC and TECG to operate as the central control agency for the exercise.
(3) Assign evaluators, to include the senior evaluator, and ensure that those evaluators are properly trained.
(4) Develop the general exercise scenario taking into account any objectives/ events prescribed by the EC.
(5) Arrange for all resources to include: training areas, airspace, aggressor forces, and other required support.

I

Individual Readiness. The individual training readiness of each Marine is measured by the number of individual events required and completed for the rank or billet currently held.

Individual Training. Training that applies to individual Marines. Examples include rifle qualifications and HMMWV driver licensing.

Individual Training Standards (ITS). Specifies training tasks and standards for each MOS or specialty within the Marine Corps. In most cases, once an MOS or community develops a T&R, the ITS order will be cancelled. However, most communities will probably fold a large portion of their ITS into their new T&R manual.

M

Marine Corps Combat Readiness and Evaluation System (MCCRES). An evaluation system designed to provide commanders with a comprehensive set of mission performance standards from which training programs can be developed; and through which the efficiency and effectiveness of training can be evaluated. The Ground T&R Program will eventually replace MCCRES.

Marine Corps Ground Training and Readiness (T&R) Program. The T&R Program is the Marine Corps' primary tool for planning and conducting training, for planning and conducting training evaluation, and for assessing training readiness. The program will provide the commander with standardized programs of instruction for units within the ground combat, combat support, and combat service support communities. It consolidates the ITS, CTS, METL and other individual and unit training management tools. T&R is a program of standards that systematizes commonly accepted skills, is open to innovative change, and above all, tailors the training effort to the unit's mission. Further, T&R serves as a training guide and provides commanders an immediate assessment of unit combat readiness by assigning a CRP to key training events. In short, the T&R Program is a building block approach to training that maximizes flexibility and produces the best-trained Marines possible.

Mission Essential Task(s) MET(s). A MET is a collective task in which an organization must be proficient in order to accomplish an appropriate portion of its wartime mission(s). MET listings are the foundation for the T&R manual; all events in the T&R manual support a MET.

Mission Essential Task List (METL). Descriptive training document that provides units a clear, war fighting focused description of collective actions necessary to achieve wartime mission proficiency. The service-level METL, that which is used as the foundation of the T&R manual, is developed using Marine Corps doctrine, Operational Plans, T/Os, UJTL, UNTL, and MCTL. For community based T&R Manuals, an occupational field METL is developed to focus the community's collective training standards. Commanders develop their unit METL from the service-level METL, operational plans, contingency plans, and SOPs.

Mission Performance Standards (MPS). Criteria that specify mission and functional area unit proficiency standards for combat, combat support and combat service support units. They include tasks, conditions, standards, evaluator instruction, and key indicators. MPS are contained within the MCCRES volumes. The MCCRES volumes are being replaced by T&R Manuals. Collective Events will replace MPS.

O

Operational Readiness (DoD, NATO). OR is the capability of a unit/formation, ship, weapon system, or equipment to perform the missions or functions for which it is organized or designed. May be used in a general sense or to express a level or degree of readiness.

P

Performance step. Performance steps are included in the components of an Individual T&R Event. They are the major procedures (i.e., actions) a unit Marine must accomplish to perform an individual event to standard. They describe the procedure the task performer must take to perform the task under operational conditions and provide sufficient information for a task performer to perform the procedure. (May necessitate identification of supporting steps, procedures, or actions in outline form.) Performance steps follow a logical progression and should be followed sequentially, unless otherwise stated. Normally, performance steps are listed only for 1000-level individual events (those that are taught in the entry-level MOS school). Listing performance steps is optional if the steps are already specified in a published reference.

Prerequisite Event. Prerequisites are the academic training and/or T&R events that must be completed prior to attempting the event.

R

Readiness (DoD). Readiness is the ability of US military forces to fight and meet the demands of the national military strategy. Readiness is the synthesis of two distinct but interrelated levels:
    (a) Unit readiness--The ability to provide capabilities required by combatant commanders to execute assigned missions. This is derived from the ability of each unit to deliver the outputs for which it was designed.
    (b) Joint readiness--The combatant commander's ability to integrate and synchronize ready combat and support forces to execute assigned missions.

S

Section Skill Tasks. Section Skills are those competencies directly related to unit functioning. They are group rather than individual in nature, and require participation by a section (S-1, S-2, S-3, etc...).

Simulation Training. Simulators provide the additional capability to develop and hone core and core plus skills. Accordingly, the development of simulator training events for appropriate T&R syllabi can help maintain valuable combat resources while reducing training time and cost. Therefore, in cases where simulator fidelity and capabilities are such that simulator training closely matches that of actual training events, T&R Manual developers may include the option of using simulators to accomplish the training. CRP credit will be earned for E-coded simulator events based on assessment of relative training event performance.

Standard. A standard is a statement that establishes criteria for how well a task or learning objective must be performed. The standard specifies how well, completely, or accurately a process must be performed or product produced. For higher-level collective events, it describes why the event is being done and the desired end-state of the event. Standards become more specific for lower-level events and outline the accuracy, time limits, sequencing, quality, product, process, restrictions, etc..., that indicate the minimum acceptable level of performance required of the event. At a minimum, both collective and individual training standards consist of a task, the condition under which the task is to be performed, and the evaluation criteria that will be used to verify that the task has been performed to a satisfactory level.

Sustainment Training. Periodic retraining or demonstration of an event required maintaining the minimum acceptable level of proficiency or capability required to accomplish a training objective. Sustainment training goes beyond the entry-level and is designed to maintain or further develop proficiency in a given set of skills.

Systems Approach to Training (SAT). An orderly process for analyzing, designing, developing, implementing, and evaluating a unit's training program to ensure the unit, and the Marines of that unit acquire the knowledge and skills essential for the successful conduct of the unit's wartime missions.

T

Training Task. This describes a direct training activity that pertains to an individual Marine. A task is composed of 3 major components: a description of what is to be done, a condition, and a standard.

Technical Exercise Controller (TEC). The TEC is appointed by the ED, and usually comes from his staff or a subordinate command. The TEC is the senior evaluator within the TECG and should be of equal or higher grade than the commander(s) of the unit(s) being evaluated. The TEC is responsible for ensuring that the evaluation is conducted following the instructions contained in this order and MCO 1553.3A. Specific T&R Manuals are used as the source for evaluation criteria.

Tactical Exercise Control Group (TECG). A TECG is formed to provide subject matter experts in the functional areas being evaluated. The benefit of establishing a permanent TECG is to have resident, dedicated evaluation authority experience, and knowledgeable in evaluation technique. The responsibilities and functions of the TECG include:
    (1) Developing a detailed exercise scenario to include the objectives and events prescribed by the EC/ED in the exercise LOI;
    (2) Conducting detailed evaluator training prior to the exercise;
    (3) Coordinating and controlling role players and aggressors;
    (4) Compiling the evaluation data submitted by the evaluators and submitting required results to the ED;
    (5) Preparing and conducting a detailed exercise debrief for the evaluated unit(s).

Training Plan. Training document that outlines the general plan for the conduct of individual and collective training in an organization for specified periods of time.

U

Unit CRP. Unit CRP is a percentage of the E-coded collective events that support the unit METL accomplished by the unit. Unit CRP is the average of all MET CRP.

Unit Evaluation. All units in the Marine Corps must be evaluated, either formally or informally, to ensure they are capable of conducting their combat mission. Informal evaluations should take place during all training events.

The timing of formal evaluations is critical and should, when appropriate, be directly related to the units' operational deployment cycle. Formal evaluations should take place after the unit has been staffed with the majority of its personnel, has had sufficient time to train to individual and collective standards, and early enough in the training cycle so there is sufficient time to correctly identified weaknesses prior to deployment. All combat units, and unit task organized for combat require formal evaluations prior to operational deployments.

Unit Training Management (UTM). Unit training management is the use of the SAT and Marine Corps training principles in a manner that maximizes training results and focuses the training priorities of the unit on its wartime mission. UTM governs the major peacetime training activity of the Marine Corps and applies to all echelons of the Total Force.

W

Waived Event. An event that is waived by a commanding officer when in his or her judgment, previous experience or related performance satisfies the requirement of a particular event.

www.ingramcontent.com/pod-product-compliance
Lightning Source LLC
Chambersburg PA
CBHW080908290526
45795CB00007BA/2458